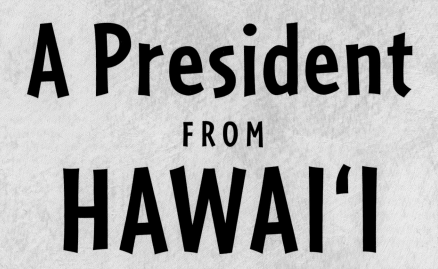

A President

FROM

HAWAI'I

Dr. Terry Carolan and Joanna Carolan

illustrated by Elizabeth Zunon

CANDLEWICK PRESS

"When I look back on my years in Hawaii, I realize how truly lucky I was to have been raised there."
— Barack Obama, Panahou Bulletin, *fall 1999*

PRESIDENT OBAMA was born in Hawai'i,
a first in America's history.
A **kama'aina** is a Hawai'i-born resident,
and Barack Obama is our first **kama'aina** president.

In Hawaiian culture, tradition plays a big part.
Living with **aloha** means giving from the heart.
It is a gesture of **aloha** to give a flower **lei.**
Showing kindness always is the **aloha** way.

"That's why we pass on the values of empathy and kindness to our children by living them."
—Barack Obama, Chicago, Illinois, 6/15/08

Is it true you can see a rainbow every day?
Let's go to Hawai'i and check it out.
Let's see what it's all about.

O`AHU
The Gathering Place

KAUA`I
The Garden Isle

Honolulu

NI`IHAU
The Forbidden Isle

A chain of islands makes up our fiftieth state.
Count the main ones – there are eight.
The capital of Hawai'i is Honolulu,
a large city on the island of O'ahu.

MOLOKA`I
The Friendly Isle

MAUI
The Valley Isle

LĀNA`I
The Pineapple Isle

KAHO`OLAWE
The Target Isle

HAWAI`I
The Big Island

President Obama grew up there in Makiki,
a couple of miles from the famous Waikiki.
In high school, he lived in an apartment
and scooped ice cream at the rate of two dollars
and forty cents.

When his homework was **pau,** or done,
he would shoot hoops with friends or bodysurf for fun.

HAVE **FUN** ON WAIKIKI BEACH

Here is where our president went to school.

Studying hard and getting good grades is very cool.

When someone is smart, we say they are **akamai.**

Barack Obama is one **akamai** guy.

Some of Hawai'i's history is sad,
but good things happened along with the bad.

Mana is what Hawaiians call divine spirit or power.
They believe it can be found in every person, rock, and flower.

Hawai'i had a monarchy, which was taken away,
but the people's **mana** was strong, and it still is today.

Lokahi is another important thing;
it's like striving for harmony when we sing.
Lokahi means looking for ways to agree,
finding the path to create unity.
Lokahi is working together as one;
it takes teamwork, patience, and cooperation.

*"On this day, we gather because we have chosen hope
over fear, unity of purpose over conflict and discord."*
—Barack Obama, inaugural address, 1/20/09

"It must be about what we can do together."
—Barack Obama, Springfield, Illinois, 2/10/07

"No frontier is beyond our reach when we're united, and not divided."
—Barack Obama, Washington, D.C., 1/28/08

"*I think about my grandmother. . . . She's the one who taught me about hard work. She's the one who put off buying a new car or a new dress for herself so that I could have a better life. She poured everything she had into me.*"
—Barack Obama, Democratic National Convention, Denver, Colorado, 8/28/08

But whether we are Christian, Jewish, Muslim, Hindu, or followers of Buddha,
Hawaiian culture tells us to honor our elders, our **kupuna.**

Our **kupuna** give us guidance, comfort, and affection,
just as our president's **tūtū** helped him find the right direction.

"We look out for one another . . . we deal with each other with courtesy and respect, and most importantly . . . when you come from Hawaii, you start understanding that what's on the surface, what people look like, that doesn't determine who they are."
— Barack Obama, Honolulu, 8/8/08

We are taught to treat everyone as family, **'ohana,**
even if they have a funny name, like Barack Obama!

Mahalo is one of the first words we are taught.
It means respect and thank you. We say it a lot.
Anyone older is called Auntie or Uncle when you're small.
And each of our **keiki** is cherished by us all.

The **'aina,** the land, is very important here.
Especially on an island, every part is dear.
Malama means preserving our island's fragile beauty.
Protecting and caring for the **'aina** is our duty.

Duty and responsibility: **kuleana** is what we say.
It's our **kuleana** to pitch in every day.
And when we help each other, it's a lot more fun.
Kokua means we work together to get something done.
Turn off the TV, look around, and get involved.
We need lots of **kokua** to get our problems solved.

"Growing up in Hawaii, not only do you appreciate the natural beauty, but there is a real ethic of concern for the land that dates back to the native Hawaiians."
—Barack Obama, U.S. News & World Report, *5/30/08*

See how everyone pulls together at a **hukilau**?
Our country needs all of us to pull together now.
You can help by showing **aloha,** rain or shine,
sharing your smile or a shaka sign.

Pono means fair, just, and good,
with everything going the way it should.
Ho'oponopono is working things out.
Resolving conflict, talking, listening, forgiving – that's what it's about.

We can be smarter, work harder, to be more **akamai.**
We can find agreement, **lokahi,** if we try.
We can preserve, protect, take care – everywhere **malama** –
and give our best **kokua** to President Obama!

*"That's the power of hope — to imagine, and then
to work for, what had seemed impossible before."*
— Barack Obama, Des Moines, Iowa, 12/27/07

GLOSSARY

'aina the land

akamai smart, clever, skilled, expert

aloha love; used as a greeting, to mean either hello or good-bye

ho'oponopono working things out, resolving conflict

hukilau community net fishing; leaves tied to a rope are used to drive fish into the net

kama'aina the Hawaiian word for native-born; also means host and is used when referring to Hawai'i residents

keiki child

kokua help, assistance, support

kuleana right, privilege; duty, responsibility

kupuna ancestor, grandparent, respected elder

lei a garland or necklace made from flowers, shells, leaves, or other materials; given as a symbol of affection or respect and to acknowledge special occasions

lokahi unity, harmony, agreement, accord

mahalo respect; gratitude; thank you

malama care, protection

mana divine spirit or power; Hawaiians believe it dwells in all living beings and natural objects

'ohana family

pau complete, finished, done

pono fair, just, good

tūtū grandparent

For Danny
T. C. and J. C.

To the ever-swaying palm trees, warm breezes, and tropical
flowers of my home; you are forever on my mind.
E. Z.

Text copyright © 2012 by Terence J. Carolan and Joanna F. Carolan
Illustrations copyright © 2012 by Elizabeth Zunon

p. 2: women holding Hawaii sign by Ablestock.com/Photos.com. pp. 3, 14, 17: Obama family snapshots used by permission of the family. pp. 3, 13, 17: bamboo frame illustrations by Joanna Carolan. p. 4: woman stringing lei by Maka and Iwalani Herrod. p. 5: Obama wearing a lei by AP/Alex Brandon. p. 6: beach by Ablestock.com /Photos.com; license plate by Joanna Carolan/Robin Pearl Graphics; restaurant logo by Rainbow Drive-In. p. 8: Obama playing basketball by Laura Kong; Obama bodysurfing by AP/Alex Brandon; Waikiki poster by Robin Pearl Graphics; Diamondhead landscape by Niko Vujevic/Photos.com. p. 10: newspaper images by the *Honolulu Star-Bulletin*, *The Honolulu Advertiser*, and *Commercial Advertiser*. p. 11: portrait of Princess Ka'iulani by E. Chickering. p. 13: hula dancers by the Polynesian Cultural Center. p. 18: The Reef Is Alive poster by saveourseas.org. pp. 18–19: photographs of signs by Joanna Carolan. p. 20: *hukilau* by Bebe Nichols. p. 21: Obama at Camp Lejeune by U.S. Marine Corps/Lance Cpl. Michael J. Ayotte.

First edition 2012

Library of Congress Cataloging-in-Publication Data

Carolan, Dr. Terry
A president from Hawai'i / Dr. Terry Carolan and Joanna Carolan ; illustrated by Elizabeth Zunon. – 1st ed.
p. cm.
ISBN 978-0-7636-5230-2 (hardcover)
ISBN 978-0-7636-6282-0 (paperback)
1. Obama, Barack – Childhood and youth – Juvenile literature.
2. Obama, Barack – Homes and haunts – Hawaii – Juvenile literatuare.
I. Carolan, Joanna F. II. Title.
E908.3.C368 2012
973.932092 – dc23 [B]   2011048107

12 13 14 15 16 17 TLF 10 9 8 7 6 5 4 3 2 1

Printed in Dongguan, Guangdong, China

This book was typeset in Cafeteria and Gill Sans.
The illustrations were done in oil and collage.

Candlewick Press
99 Dover Street
Somerville, Massachusetts 02144

visit us at www.candlewick.com